BEST WISHES,

Otto Lang.

Around the World in 90 Years

Images from My Life's Journey

Otto Lang

ISBN 1-58619-017-2

Around the World in 90 Years
Copyright 2000 by Otto Lang
Published by Elton-Wolf Publishing
2505 Second Avenue, Suite 515
Seattle, Washington 98121
For information: (206) 748-0345
www.elton-wolf.com

Library of Congress 00-105636
Printed in China through Palace Press International, San Francisco, California
Designed by TMA Ted Mader Associates, Seattle, Washington

The Journey

Foreword

Working in my studio in the afternoon on New Year's Eve, 1999, my attention was drawn intermittently to the television in the corner. The network news was following the turning of the new year in major cities around the world as it crept slowly westward: Tokyo, Bombay, Moscow, Berlin, Paris, London, and Lisbon. I must admit that with all of the hype and concern surrounding Y2K I, like many people, had not really stopped to contemplate in any significant way this last century of the millennium which was about to pass into the night, giving way to a bold new one.

Spread out before me on my editing table was a wondrous collection of photographs captured from many corners of the world and taken during the twentieth century by a very remarkable man, Otto Lang. Caught up in the moment and inspired by this "visual time capsule," I allowed myself a brief moment of retrospection of the last one hundred years.

There is little argument that this century has seen the greatest acceleration of human achievement since the dawn of man. We built the car, flew the airplane, set human feet on a celestial body, conquered diseases, replaced the human heart, and cloned a sheep, to name but a few miracles of man. We also had the two most brutal, destructive wars in man's history; endure to this day bloody regional conflicts; and from the best scientific minds, have created weapons of mass destruction that can end all life on earth as we know it.

Although I only came on the scene in the second half of this century (1952), members of my generation are fortunate enough to have experienced through our parents and their generation some degree of appreciation of those times and events earlier in the century that shaped the world we live in today.

At the age of ninety-two, the life of Otto Lang has spanned virtually the entire twentieth century. Born in the tumultuous region of the Balkans shortly before the breakout of World War I, he came to know at a very young age the horrors of war. So too, did he come to appreciate the joy and wonder of life, growing up in a loving family and close-knit community, surrounded by the beauty of unspoiled nature.

His love of the outdoors would eventually lead him to commit his considerable athletic skills to the development of downhill skiing, becoming an instructor in Tirol, Austria. Ultimately it was his restless and adventurous spirit that would bring him to the United States, where here, he would become one of the major forces in the development of downhill skiing. They say that success occurs the moment preparedness meets opportunity. For Otto, that moment arrived when he met and became lifelong friends with Twentieth Century Fox Films president and famed producer, Darryl F. Zanuck in Sun Valley, Idaho in 1940. It was from this relationship that Otto began a long and successful career in film, that would among other acclaim, bestow upon him four Academy Award nominations for his films.

As fate would have it, it was our love of photography and the spirit of adventure that brought Otto and me together. As we began to work on his book project, little by little I came to realize the abundance of not only his talent as an athlete and gifted visual artist, but even more, his insatiable thirst for life and his compassion for all humankind.

Assembling the images for this book was no easy task, for Otto has built an impressive library of photographs that span the globe and many decades of this century. Although Otto's professional career was in filmmaking, it wasn't long after I began to edit his images that it made sense to me that his gifted eye and his love of people and places would so easily translate to the still image. I think that of all the many worthy aspects of this book, the most important to me is that Otto has captured moments in time, people and places as they were years and decades ago. So, as we move now into this new era, the twentieth century ever more a fading memory, *Around the World in 90 Years* becomes one man's living testament to a very remarkable time in human history.

Bruce Heinemann
Seattle, Washington
Spring 2000

Introduction

According to scientific calculations and research statistics, planet Earth thus far is the only inhabited celestial body known to us. It is 4.6 to 5 billion years old, give or take a few million. The total landmass is 196,140,000 square miles. One-third of it is terra firma and two-thirds water: oceans, lakes, and rivers. Its composite weight is 6,586,000,000,000,000,000,000,000 tons. Mind boggling!

Through history's passage, planet Earth has been segmented into seven continents by learned geographers and intrepid explorers, to wit: Africa, Antarctica, Asia, Australia, Europe, North America, and South America. Its population is approximately six billion, inexorably growing by leaps and bounds.

At one point or another, I set foot on six of these continents, missing Antarctica. However, that was only a minuscule part of the world I came to know, since each continent was subdivided into a multitude of countries with a myriad of large cities, small towns and villages, different nationalities, racial separations, and varied religious followings. Therefore, this compact booklet, with a limited number of photographs and annotations, lacks in scope what I wished it to be when I began to sort out the images of particular poignancy to me. There were too many in the vast reservoir of original transparencies and negatives accumulated through my roaming around this globe in ninety years.

In the pursuit of earning my livelihood, I began as a ski instructor with the legendary Hannes Schneider at St. Anton am Arlberg, Austria, in 1929. Subsequently, in 1935, when I migrated to the United States, I founded and directed three ski schools in the Pacific Northwest at Mt. Rainier, Mt. Baker, and Mt. Hood. In 1939, I moved on to Sun Valley, Idaho, in the same capacity, which eventually led me into my second career as a Hollywood film director and producer. In fact, the most rewarding opportunities for taking photographs in a haphazard fashion occurred to me during my search for suitable locations to shoot feature films and documentaries in foreign countries.

Undoubtedly, a turning point in this respect came in 1958 when, just for a lark, I entered two of my 35mm color slides in *The Saturday Review* magazine's annual world photo contest. Lo and behold, to my total surprise, one of my slides entitled "Blind Beggar," taken in Sri Lanka (then Ceylon), won the grand prize among circa 9,000 contestants. The other entry, "Rainy Day in Florence," also placed among the top ten.

Winning this competition was definitely an added incentive to perfect my aspirations in this demanding avocation of still photography.

I used a number of different format cameras, lenses and brands of film during my extensive travels to follow. My collection of images grew to a point where I fretted what to do with this surfeit of material stored in dozens of albums. I toyed with the idea of possibly someday in the future coming out with a book of photographs, still a nebulous concept in my mind.

To my regret, I kept no records concerning the technical data of these originals.

Fortuitously, the spark for a book was ignited when I browsed through a published portfolio of photographs by Bruce Heinemann, a first-rate artist in his field, primarily dedicated to capture nature's scenic beauty and bounty with singular insight. I contacted him by phone and invited him to have lunch with me, which he graciously accepted. Afterward, looking at the collection of photographs at my home, I bluntly confessed to him that I wanted to do a book, cloning his in concept, format, quality of printing, and overall presentation.

Even though I had recently published my memoir, *A Bird of Passage*, with Falcon Press in Montana, garnering excellent reviews and public acceptance, I realized that putting out a book of photographs was a bird of a different plumage. To accomplish this, I needed the help and expertise Bruce could provide to me, if he were willing to do so.

It was my good fortune that after seeing the quality and variety of my collection, he consented to become a vital part in the development of this project.

On the spur of the moment, I suggested the title *Around the World in 90 Years*, which intrigued Bruce, and off to work we went with a handshake on a proposed business association, which has matured into a close personal friendship.

After many preliminary discussions, we agreed that this would not be a manual for aspiring photographers, as to what lenses, films and f-stops to use and, also, hints in regard to improving the composition of a prospective tableau. Mine would be simply kaleidoscopic glimpses of one photographer's peregrinations around the globe. It would be a tribute to the "family of man" and beauty of nature surrounding us.

Bruce also introduced me to Ted Mader who, in turn, brought me together with his graphic design associates, a group of highly talented young people.

They would create the design of the book's cover and finalize the layout and juxtaposition of photographs and text.

To Ted Mader, Cindy Dieter, Fritz Rothman, my profoundest thanks for their unflagging interest in this project and bringing it to fruition.

Also, many thanks to Dave Moffett, his brother Bill and sister Loren, for their genuine interest in getting this book into print, as was my dear friend Christy Hill of Vail, Colorado.

Maestro Gerard (Jerry) Schwarz and Jody his stylish spouse, and their two children Gaby and Julian have given me their constant spiritual support in carrying on with this project.

So have Emmett Watson, Richard Zanuck, David Brown, Pamela McClusky, and Robert Cameron.

And of course, Bruce Heinemann, my partner and friend, without whose help this book might have never materialized.

Most of all I want to thank June Campbell from all my heart, for having stood by me through all seasons for fifteen years and for her invaluable suggestions during the protracted genesis of this opus.

Otto Lang
Seattle, Washington
August 2000

Dedication

With love, to Sinclair (Sinnie ✝, 1990) and our sons Peter and Mark, who so bravely endured my long absences and also occasionally shared my adventurous journeys around the globe.

Peter, Sinnie, Mark, and Otto
Sun Valley Archives, 1948

Chapter One

My life's European odyssey began on January 21, 1908 with my birth in Tésanj, a small village with a predominantly Muslim population, near Sarajevo, the capital of Bosnia.

My mother was of Croatian ancestry, whereas my father, born in Austria, was an officer in Kaiser Franz Joseph I's military, who had annexed and integrated Bosnia into its vast Austro-Hungarian Empire.

We, our parents and my three sisters, weathered World War I triggered by the assassination of Archduke Ferdinand I, at Sarajevo. At war's end in 1918, we moved on to Salzburg in Austria.

It was at Salzburg that I grew into manhood and therefore look upon this city as my hometown and Austria as my fatherland.

That is, until in 1935 when I migrated to the U.S.A. and was sworn in as a "naturalized citizen" on November 21, 1941, in Los Angeles, California Citizen Certificate 5258256.

Europe

Salzburg, Austria
City view with fortress Hohen Salzburg. Ever since I first set foot on its soil, Salzburg left an indelible imprint in my memory as a magical city.

(left)

Marionette Theatre
One of my first encounters with the "visual arts" as a ten-year-old youngster was Salzburg's Marionette Theatre. It has grown from an affordable children's diversion into a highly artistic presentation for all ages, of dramatic plays, opera and even classic ballet.

The cast of *Die Fledermaus* by Johann Strauss—a lighthearted Viennese musical treat.

(above)

"There is very little in the movements of the human body that can not be duplicated by our marionettes.

This is my life. I'm up here on the bridge above the stage, working in almost every performance. It can be physically very strenuous and emotionally draining. I love every minute of it."

Gretl Aicher
Master Puppeteer, Artistic Director

11

Vienna, Austria

The capital of Austria in which
the Hapsburg royalty lived in
palaces rivaling Versailles. They
dined from gold plates, danced
to minuets composed by Mozart
and Haydn, but also felt the
impact of a rebellious young
composer, his name: Herr
Ludwig van Beethoven.

Not in my wildest dreams did
I anticipate to return to Vienna
and Bonn, Germany in the
distant career as a filmmaker,
to shoot a biography of this
illustrious composer, *Beethoven:
Ordeal and Triumph.*

It featured the Boston Symphony
Orchestra with Erich Leinsdorf
its conductor and the renowned
concert pianist Claude Frank
portraying Beethoven.

The theme of the film was
Beethoven's ordeal in over-
coming his progressive deafness
and eventual triumph in leaving
us a legacy of the finest
musical offerings by a composer
considered virtually deaf.

The film was shown on April 26,
1966 in primetime nationwide
on the ABC-TV network and
was exceedingly well received
by viewers and highly praised
by TV and film critics.

In 1885, Jules Jouant, a
contemporary of Auguste
Rodin, created this somewhat
idealistic and heroic bronze
likeness of Beethoven.

London, England
Arguably the most cultural and
civilized city in the world.

Big Ben with red bus.
(right)

Mounted guard.
(left)

Tall Tales

In 1826, the Viceroy of Egypt gifted the Emperor of France with an obelisk, one of the twins, originally guarding the entrance of the Sacred Temple of God Amon at Luxor. It was a monolith hewn from granite, seventy feet tall, weighing 230 tons, about 3,300 years old and liberally inscribed with mysterious hieroglyphics, still undeciphered at that time. With ingenuity, levers, pulleys, stout cables and hordes of manpower, it was boxed into a wooden crate, then loaded onto and barged down the Nile River to Alexandria.

From there it was hauled by a steamboat on a journey of many months, across the Mediterranean, bypassing Sicily, the Rock of Gibraltar, around Spain and on the Cherbourg and Le Havre to meet the Seine River. From there it was towed to Paris, its final destination near a landing site known as the "Place de La Concorde." Here it stands now proudly, after a ten-year journey, gracing one of the world's most magnificent public plazas.

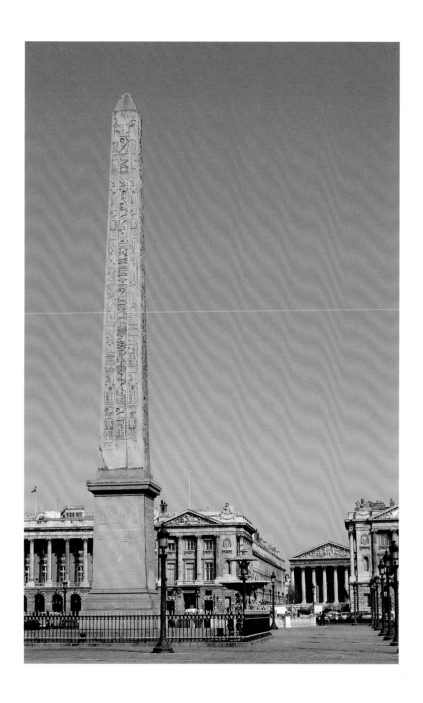

Place de La Concorde—Obelisk
Paris, France.

(left)

Origin of Obelisk—Egypt
Luxor, Temple of Amon.

(opposite)

Coincidentally, about the same time another tall visitor arrived in Paris, also a gift from the Viceroy of Egypt to King Charles II of France. It was a live female giraffe, born in the darkest of Africa, walked to Kartum in the Sudan, there entrusted into the care of Monsieur Etienne Saint-Hilaire, a dedicated French naturalist and director of the "Jardin Des Plantes," the local zoo, in Paris. She was floated down the Nile on a native fellucah and walked around the occasional cataracts of this river until she reached Alexandria.

Here, on a specially constructed barge with a hole cut in the upper deck to stick out her head on a long neck, she journeyed to Marseille. From there in a triumphant overland march for two months accompanied by a colorful retenue of animal handlers, she progressed in stages across France, greeted and followed by a mob of enthralled citizens, who had never seen a live giraffe before. Zarafa, as she was named, endeared herself all over Europe and was covered by the press worldwide. She settled down to a long-lived residency at the Paris Zoo.

Then in 1899, Gustave Eiffel, a French engineer came along. It took him two years to design and supervise the building of a wondrous structure in steel. One thousand feet high and accessible to its very top it was named the Eiffel Tower. It was built in honor of a pending visitor, the Prince of Wales, Edward VII. Many stodgy Parisians and blasé art connoisseurs looked upon it as an architectural monstrosity, not worthy of their fair city. Some branded it as ugly, resembling the ungainly physical proportions of a giraffe notwithstanding Zarafa's legendary popularity, who had long since died.

How wrong they were! The Eiffel Tower, nowadays acclaimed as a masterpiece in iron structure, meticulously maintained and treasured by Parisians, has become the logo signature of the city and a most popular tourist attraction.

Eiffel Tower.

(left)

Zarafa the Giraffe.

(opposite)

West Berlin—with a ray of hope.

Berlin, Germany

When in 1954, during the filming of *Night People* for Twentieth
Century Fox, I saw the total
devastation brought upon this
city and Germany by the aerial
bombing during World War II.
I was shocked beyond belief.

East Berlin—doomed by Stalin's
communist regime.

Greece

Ancient Greece, one of the cradles of civilization with its diverse offerings of serene landscapes, antiquities, and idyllic islands.

Delphi Antiquities

I found no lovelier landscape in all of Greece, then the site occupied by the well-known "oracle" of this ancient country.

Heavily damaged by repeated earthquakes, it still offers a large repository of the finest Greek architecture with its configuration of religious shrines, temples, theatre and stadium.

(left)

One of the precariously perched monasteries at Meteora near Saloniki. It is inhabited by monks of many nationalities, celibate and dedicated to prayer and working around the clock.

(right)

Athens

The Acropolis at Athens, honoring Zeus and other deities in the pantheon of Greek mythology. The Parthenon, dedicated to Athena (Goddess of War) is the epitome of a classic architectural edifice minus the magnificent marble friezes, spirited away by the Brits to be displayed at their London museum.

My endeavor was to get an image devoid of camera-toting tourists populating the foreground. It took a while and patience.

(left)

To me, there is a similar beauty in this grove of venerable olive trees, aside from being a staple food supplement.

(left)

Peloponnese, Greece
The island of Poros.

(right)

Italy

For all of Europe's northern population, Italy beckons like a mecca for sun lovers, with cities such as Florence, past the rural Tuscany, on to Rome and fabled Naples.

Siena, Italy
A flock of female fledglings.

(left)

Florence, Italy
"Piazza Della Signoria" with all its impressive statuary.

(right)

Florence, Italy
A classic sight of the city and its *Ponte Vecchio.*

(above)

Rome, Italy
Fountain of the Dolphin and Turtle. One of my favorite fountains expressing the exuberant joy of life.

(left)

Rainy Day in Florence
Waiting for the sun to come out, I found nothing better to do than to take this picture, right out of the hotel's front door.

(right)

Switzerland

A citadel of "neutrality," world banking, mother of posh winter resorts, and also inventors of the cuckoo clock.

Matterhorn and Mt. Blanc, two of the most revered alpine peaks.

Turkey

Istanbul is the kind of a city perfectly fit as the background for an oriental fairy tale or a present-day suspense film such as *Topkapi*, directed by Jules Dassin or the riveting spy melodrama *Five Fingers*, which I produced. Oddly though, Istanbul, by straddling the Bosporus, the dividing line between two continents, has a firm foothold on European soil, while the other foot and main body of Turkey is solidly planted in Asia. The combination of such opposite cultures and mores, makes it an even more intriguing city.

Göreme and Ürgip

Should one wish to build one's own condominium, just pick a rock of hardened volcanic ash and mud, to chisel out a habitat with a view.

(above)

33

Mausoleum, Ankara

The mausoleum for Kemal Ataturk, the dynamic revolutionary leader, who catapulted Turkey into the twentieth century (ca. 1930), with many drastic political reforms.

He banished the Ottoman red *fez* traditionally worn by men and *chador* for women, a most unbecoming black shroud, covering every particle of bare skin and hair, except for a narrow slit for the eyes.

The Turkish women—and men welcomed the change, while the Islamic clerics deplored it.

Mausoleum honor guard.

(right)

Yugoslavia

My attachment to Yugoslavia
remains unchanged. It is my
fervent hope that the day must
and will come when its racially
and religiously varied population
will learn to live with one another.
peacefully and productively.
I have visited it many times
and crisscrossed by automobile
in every direction. It is a country
of singular beauty and rich in
natural resources.

Sarajevo, the capital of Bosnia. a
beguiling city of many nationalities,
cultures, and religious affiliations
was severely damaged by many
wars but has always risen again with
a cachet of charm and glamour.

(left)

This lofty span of a bridge at
Mostar (Bosnia) was an architectural masterpiece of elegance.
built by the Ottoman invaders.
For 450 years it withstood the
ravage of wars, earthquakes
and floods until 1995, when it
was virtually destroyed by the
artillery barrage of Yugoslavia's
opposing nationalities embroiled
in a brutally fought conflict.

(above right)

Bosnian cheese vendor.

(below right)

During the last conflict, Yugoslav men tilled the killing fields and devastated the country with senseless brutality, while the women left behind stood firm to protect their homes, take care of the children, help the ailing and protect the elderly.

Bosnain woman symbolically holding up the foundations of the home.

(right)

Prizren, Kosovo
A street scene.

(left)

A Kosovar shepherd.

(above left)

"His and Hers," an eye catching glimpse on the road to Montenegro.

(below left)

Sveti Stefan
Once a thriving fishing village, now converted by the government into a picturesque, upscale resort with gambling casino.

(right)

Africa

The mystique of the African continent has remained with me from the moment I stepped off the TWA plane onto the tarmac at Léopoldville, then the capital of Colonial Belgian Congo in 1952.

I expected it to be hot and tropically humid but obviously livable judging by the milling crowds of tribal natives, professional white hunters meeting adventure-seeking clients and trophy-laden tourists getting ready to depart.

My mission was to look for suitable locations and prepare for the shooting of *White Witch Doctor*, a feature film for Twentieth Century Fox.

It would be based on a novel by Louise Stinetorf, depicting her experiences as a medical missionary in the hinterlands of this country.

I brought this book to Darryl F. Zanuck's attention; he bought it and assigned me to produce the film.

Susan Hayward would portray the missionary, and Robert Mitchum the part of a purveyor of exotic animals for the zoos of the world and also a gold-grubbing prospector.

All this blended into a Hollywood inspired love story, not contained in the original novel. Well fortified with a prodigious amount of research material, I started out on a lengthy journey, covering the width and length of the continent, from Léopoldville to Stanleyville up north and hence east to Nairobi, Kenya.

It was a wondrous journey by various means of transportation. We saw spectacular scenery, fascinating native villages and peoples, and an abundance

of fauna and flora. Some of these eventually would be included in our film.

Oddly enough, the village and tribe I chose for our main location shoot was the very first one that I visited, only a short flight from Léopoldville.

It was the tribe of the Bakubas, ruled by a hereditary succession of kings with a highly developed culture in various crafts, colorful costumes, spectacular dances and masks.

Chapter Two

Mbopey Mabintsh Ma-Kee
The King of the Bakubas in his full ceremonial regalia.

In 1952, he actively participated in the filming of *White Witch Doctor* at Mushenge, the capital of his domain, surrounded by his royal court functionaries, 350 wives, and innumerable children.

Of course, he had to be "doubled" by a Hollywood actor in the more intimate dialogue scenes and close-ups, filmed on the studio set.

After his death in 1969 and the take-over of the former Belgian Congo by a communist tainted regime, embroiled in bitter internecine fighting, the Bakuba tribe fell by the wayside and virtually vanished with all its tradition and artistry lost.

The wooden statuettes of every reigning king, about twenty-eight inches high, carved in a prescribed foreshortened archaic style, were sought after by collectors and museums worldwide. The one shown here, happens to be mine.

The Wagenia tribe near Kisangani (formerly Stanleyville) built and used these rickety walkways to anchor their conical fish traps, on a side channel of the Congo River. It has kept them well fed and commercially solvent.

(left)

An African Nimrod with his inseparable companion, a Basenji dog without a bark, doing it the old-fashioned way with a bow and poison-tipped arrows.

(right)

Women waiting for the paddle steamer to arrive. Notice the pile of wood as the sole fuel for the boat.

(above left)

Zebras grazing—a peaceful dawn in the African veld.

(below left)

The Mangbetu Tribe near Isoro (formerly Paulis) bind the head of their infants until it reaches the elongated shape, considered beautiful, or "cool" as we would say nowadays.

(right)

Egypt

Egypt is a country of pharaonic grandeur, with its remains of historic edifices and colorful past.

Through my affiliation with Twentieth Century Fox I was designated to shoot background footage for *Justine* a film based on one of Lawrence Durrell's novels. Also, as a trade-off with the Egyptian government to permit us to do so, we would produce a promotional documentary film.

All went well until we were caught in the maws of the 1973 Arab-Israeli War, but that's another story.

Justine was a box-office disappointment. For political reasons the documentary film was never edited.

To me, Egypt is one of the most photogenic countries I have encountered. I could be lured back any time.

The gift of the Nile has existed through millenniums and is still today a gift of life for all of Egypt and its people. *(left)*

During the flooding season every year it has deposited a layer of fine silt as an organic fertilizer for its agricultural fields along both banks of the river.

Also, there was a brisk flow of commercial traffic up and down its 4,000-mile-long journey from the Sudan in Africa to Alexandria on the Mediterranean Sea.

With the creation of the monumental Aswan Dam, harnessing the flow of the Nile, it supplied Egypt with billions of kilowatt in electrical power.

It also created an equally huge new body of water, named Lake Nasser.

Aside from changing noticeably the ecology of the country, it also posed the problem of salvaging a number of priceless edifices destined to disappear forever under the rising waters of this lake.

One of these was the unique Temple of Abu Simble built by Ramses II. *(right)*

By the joint financial participation and efforts of many nations (Unesco), it was cut into a myriad of blocks, meticulously numbered and charted to be fitted together again, after being raised ninety feet onto a rocky promontory.

Here you can see indigenous workmen patch the scars left by the incision and repair the cracks developed during the stones natural aging process.

A Moslem pilgrim just returned from his *hajj* to Mecca, the obligatory journey to the holiest of Islamic shrines, at least once during a believer's life span.

(left)

The camel, a Bedouin's best friend in the vastness of the desert, deserves his master's special attention.

(right)

The pyramids of Giza near Cairo,
are surely one of the great
wonders of millenniums past.

A stone quarry at the outskirts of Cairo with men harvesting blocks of stone by hand and with identical primitive tools as they have done since times long past.

I was searching for a singular picture of the pyramids brewing in my mind and found it in this gnarled old tree, that has weathered the choking sandstorms and fiery heat of the Sahara Desert through many decades.

(left)

With the head of a woman and elongated body of a lion, the sphinx has seen it all—the cavalcade of history, the rich and impoverished, the multitude of pharaohs, Roman rulers, monarchs of many countries, statesman and celebrities of modern times, all gazing up at this ageless mysterious creature in awe and puzzlement.

(right)

Chapter Three

Had it not been for the coronation of the king-to-be of Nepal, His Majesty Mahendra, Bir Bikram Shah Dev, chances are that I might have never seen parts of this fascinating continent.

His coronation scheduled for May 30, 1956, according to strict tantric rituals, set for the exact hour and minute of the chosen day, all based upon the most propitious constellation of heavenly stars, to take place at Katmandu, this country's capital.

This was to be the wellspring of the next *Cinerama, Search for Paradise*, filmed under the aegis of Lowell Thomas. He, who had brought this cinematic novelty with the three-eyed camera and wide-screen image to the public's attention, with his first film *This is Cinerama*.

Conveniently, he was assigned by President Eisenhower as the official U.S.A. envoy to attend this oriental durbar, promising much pomp and panoply, bound to attract a large delegation of monarchs, ambassadors, dignitaries, and celebrities from many foreign countries.

Based upon my long-standing friendship with Lowell, on and off the ski slopes, and track record as a filmmaker, I was invited by him to direct this film.

Hence, this selection of images from various countries in Asia, being vital participants in this search.

You may well want to ask, did we find this earthly Shangri-La? Well, yes and no!

Asia

King Mahendra's festive procession after the coronation ceremonies at Katmandu's Hanuman Temple.

A "sea of faces" avidly
following the parade led by
the royal couple high upon
a caparisoned elephant.

It may seem to be an optical illusion but wherever I turned "the eyes of Buddha" followed me.

(left)

One of the holiest of sacred shrines in Katmandu is that of the Hindu Goddess Vishnu, reclining on a bed of snakes in a pool of water, accompanied by the constant drone of the repeated prayer "Om mani padme hum."

(right)

Not too long before King
Mahendra's coronation, vintage
luxury automobiles had to be
carried and hauled over rugged
mountainous terrain to
Katmandu. There were no
roads linking India with Nepal
fit to travel by automobile.
I restaged such an episode
for our *Cinerama* film *Search
for Paradise*.

(left)

The road to Hunza, an isolated
mountain kingdom in Pakistan,
which could have been the
inspiration of the mythical
Shangri-La so vividly captured
in James Hilton's novel *Lost
Horizon*, made into a film in
1937 by Frank Capra.

(right)

The Mir of Hunza, a benevolent
ruler, father figure and judge
without recourse in disputes
among his people, holds court
surrounded by his elders and son,
heir to the throne.

(above)

Amazingly advanced learning
curriculum of students at Baltit,
the miniscule capital of Hunza,
where they are being taught four
languages: English, Urdu,
Persian, and Arabic.

A schoolroom in the sky, pitted
against towering Mt. Rakaposhi,
25,000 feet high.

(right)

The Royal Hunza Symphony
Orchestra *(left)* provides the
musical accompaniment for all
occasions, be that a festive sword
dance, *(above right)* ferocious
polo game or charming rural
picnic *(below right)*. The Rani,
wife of the Mir seated next to
him, permitted for the first
time ever to be photographed
without a veil covering her
pretty face. Renoir might have
been tempted to paint such a
pastoral tableau.

A touch of proper housekeeping
in Hong Kong.

Chinese Widow

As a rare privilege Jennifer Jones and William Holden insisted on accompanying me as the second unit director to shoot scenes in Hong Kong, in person rather than using "doubles," for Twentieth Century Fox's film *Love Is a Many Splendored Thing*.

To work with two such stellar actors, thoroughly professional and cooperative, was like a paid vacation in an exotic and vibrant environment. Hong Kong reminded me of a busy, buzzing beehive of activities with people vying for breathing and living space.

Even though Jennifer Jones, then married to David Selznik, kept much to herself, Bill Holden was the man-about-town, very popular and recognized by people on the street. He knew the best tailor in town and was welcome in the kitchen of the best Chinese chefs in Hong Kong.

As I was wont to do I never took a photograph of either Bill or Jennifer, but lucked out with one memorable photograph of an elderly Chinese lady sitting on a stone bench.

When I raised my camera to take a picture of her, she protested vehemently and held both her hands flatly against her face. After much cajoling with her in basic sign and body language she demurred, still reluctantly holding up one finger, indicating that I could take only one picture. No more!

So with the fast waning light of the sinking sun and no flash on hand, I exposed one single frame.

When I saw it developed and enlarged, I called it "Chinese Widow." I look upon it as a modest homage to one of my favorite great painters Mynherr Rembrandt Harmenszoon van Rijn.

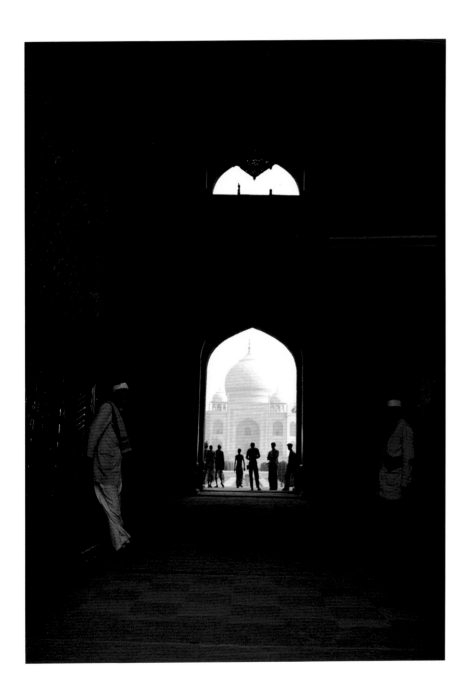

The Taj Mahal, undoubtedly one of the most photographed edifices in all of India. It was built and crafted with exquisite detail, dedicated by Shah Jahan to his beloved wife Momtaz Mahal in 1629.

Both of them are joined in death in the center of this mausoleum.

(left)

The flotilla of luxuriously appointed houseboats for rental with servants, along the shores of Dal Lake at Srinagar, the capital of Kashmir. Life here could come close to a found Shangri-la, were it not for a most destructive armed conflict raging for over thirty years between India and Pakistan to annex Kashmir.

(right)

The kingdom of Thailand (formerly Siam) has had much exposure during the past decades, mainly due to its stage and film presentations, depicting the highly romanticized and exaggerated personal relationship between King Mangkut and Anna Harriette Leonwens.

As one of the first emancipated and western oriented monarchs of the country, he imported the English governess to teach him, his crown prince Chulalonghorn, numerous wives, concubines, and dozens of the most adorable children, in European ways and mores.

It brought Thailand to the attention of a worldwide audience in theatres and movie houses, showing the beauty of the countryside, richness of palatial settings, costumes, pageantry and ceremonial functions, as an enchanted part of this universe. And so I found it to be, on my first visit—enchanting.

A Bangkok Klong traffic gridlock, with no danger of going hungry.

(right)

Bali, Indonesia
Mourners of families carrying
offerings on their way to the
traditional cremation ceremonies,
frequently taking place in Bali.
It is actually a festive celebration
of the deceased's rebirth to a
new life.

(above)

Java, Indonesia
Borobudur Buddha—While waiting for the gate to be opened and
begin filming a documentary on
the historic temple of Borobudur,
I was captivated by the serenity
of this hazy morning tableau.

(right)

Singapore Chinese Street Opera

A seasoned traveling company of Chinese thespians performs a rousing most colorful show of high drama, love and treachery, accompanied by a loud din of weird instruments; totally captivating and not easily forgotten.

(above)

Blind Beggar

My prize-winning and signature photograph of the "Blind Beggar" taken at Ceylon (now Sri Lanka), while scouting locations for *Search for Paradise*.

It was actually one of the easiest photographs taken by me, when I realized that the man was blind.

I was wearing rubber-soled boots and could move around silently, without even being noticed. It was a piece of cake from a photographer's point of view, with the subdued light of a sunless day, avoiding deep contrast shadows, that made the picture what it is.

(right)

The Philippines is another one of those fabled countries offering an incredible variety in photographic imagery.

It could also be called the land of a thousand islands, surrounding the main island, stretching from the legendary rice terraces up north at Banaue to Zamboanga, a city of seafarers, way down south.

Its history when the Japanese army chased out the American military forces from the Philippines after the bombing of Pearl Harbor is well documented. It forced General MacArthur into a dramatic escape and temporary exile. As he boarded the vessel at Corregidor he exclaimed, "I shall return." And so he did eventually, to recapture the Philippines.

Mayon Volcano

A perfectly formed cone of a volcano with the nasty habit of frequent eruptions, devastating the countryside and killing people. The last one at the turn of the twentieth century.

(left)

The Igorote tribe once primitive and feared headhunters and now more civilized rice farmers at Banaue, yet, still clinging to the beliefs and ceremonial gatherings of their ancestral leaders.

(above left)

Zamboanga

There is a large segment of people known as the "boat people," who are born, raised and living in these limited confines rarely stepping ashore.

(above right)

Preparing the soil for the rice
field is a man's job.

(above)

Planting the rice seedlings
is a woman's work.

(right)

Japan

There is no other nation I know of that "winterizes" and protects its shrubbery with a cover of decorative thatch swaddling.

In the background the castle of Osaka. one of the finest and oldest of its kind.

(left)

A *tori* at Hakone to give the landscape an added Japanese touch.

(above)

To visit Kyoto's ancient temples is part of the learning program of students at an early age.

(above)

Each temple has its "medicinal supply" of sake, a pleasant and deceptively potent beverage, stored in these handsome containers.

(right)

Winter Olympics at Hokkaido, 1972—One of my cherished memories was my official assignment as a reporter for the *San Diego Union* paper and "Copley Press National Wire Service," to cover the 1972 winter Olympics at Hokkaido. I liked this kind of work, as it gave me unrestricted access to all venues and shared living at the Olympic village quarters with all athletes.

Opening ceremony—torch carrier.
(left)

Ski Jumper—Everything that goes up, must come down, but where will he land, that is the question for you to figure out.
(opposite)

The classic ancient Tokaido road connecting Edo (now Tokyo) with Kyoto, at one time the imperial city of Japan.

The bridge was constructed without a metal nail in it and reminds me of a print by Hiroshige, one of Japan's most noted artists.

(above)

In contrast to the old bridge, here is a full-scale replica of the *Nagato*. She was Admiral Isoroku Yamamoto's flagship and built as a set for Twentieth Century Fox's film *Tora! Tora! Tora!*, one of the costliest ever made by this studio, until *Cleopatra* came along.

Due to a sudden incapacitating illness of Akira Kurosawa, the director and producer of the Japanese portion of the film depicting the preparations and successful attack on Pearl Harbor, I was chosen to take over as associate producer with two newly selected Japanese directors to replace Kurosawa.

Admiral Yamamoto, who masterminded the whole attack from his flagship, has spent a fair amount of time and studied in the U.S.A. He was fully aware of the consequences after he received the news of the successful bombing attack and decimation of the American Naval Forces, bottled up in Pearl Harbor.

Instead of jubilation he somberly predicted: "Now we have only awakened a sleeping tiger." His prognosis turned out to be correct. In 1945 Japan capitulated by signing the articles of surrender on the battleship *Missouri*, in the presence of General Douglas MacArthur.

(right)

Chapter Four

My first contact with South America was in the late spring of 1936, after a stormy winter's residence at Mt. Rainier, Washington while running my ski school.

I longed for the proverbial sunshine of California and drove straight south to Coronado Island, across the bay from San Diego, for a lengthy stay.

Tijuana, Mexico situated a few miles farther south was somewhat of a shoddy border town with a faded sheen of once-upon-a-time elegance. Nevertheless Tijuana still attracted hordes of tourists, movie stars and celebrities who mingled with the colorful populace and indulged in duty-free bargain shopping in boutiques filled with luxury goods imported from Europe.

Also, during the summer months every Sunday afternoon there was a "Fiesta Brava," commonly known as a traditional Hispanic bullfight, with imported matadors and occasionally a Mexican prodigy to partake in this century-old combat of a man fighting an angered bull.

By coincidence, I had just finished reading *Death in the Afternoon* by Ernest Hemingway, a definitive treatise on bullfighting. From it I gathered that the odds of survival are heavily stacked in favor of the matador, even though exposed to mortal danger or being maimed for life, while the bull is predestined to die in this often bloody and gruesome spectacle.

Only on rare occasions, when vociferously demanded by the public, is a bull allowed to leave the arena alive when it flatly refused to become involved in this mêlée and firmly stood still, to be shamefully dismissed, whereas a bull having shown exceptional courage and resilience is triumphantly escorted out of the arena.

All this information had aroused my interest in attending the next bullfight. As it happened, it featured one of the stellar Spanish matadors.

Although his performance, by cutting two ears as a high accolade, did not turn me on to become a dedicated aficionado, I felt more like a bewildered "gringo," with my total sympathy in favor of the tormented bull.

I did realize, however, that there were some moments of balletic proficiency in the matador's repertory of classic "veronicas" and other diversionary pirouettes with his billowing yellow cape, awaiting the bull charging at full speed, ready to impale with his sharply pointed horns any obstacle in its path.

To me it remains puzzling why this spectacle is so popular with the Hispanic population around the world.

But then, who can explain the fascination of American audiences with the preposterous and ludicrous farce of staged professional wrestling matches, with delirious fans filling large arenas to capacity.

My most haunting memory after attending this bullfight is this telltale photograph, echoing Hemingway's book *Death in the Afternoon.*"

It reminded me of the decadent times of the declining Roman Empire, when gladiators fought each other and untamed exotic animals to death for the entertainment of the Roman populace.

South America

Mexico, Yucatán

Many, many years later in 1969, I was commissioned to shoot footage for a biographical documentary film for ABC-TV, entitled *The Legend of Hernán Cortés.*

Cortés, a Spaniard, who in 1519 embarked and headed for Mexico with eleven sailing ships, 508 swordsmen, 100 sailors, 32 cross-bowmen, 13 musketeers, 10 brass cannons, 4 smaller cannons, loads of powder and cannonballs, sundry spare parts, ample food supplies, 16 horses, and a dozen dogs. His objective, to subjugate and demolish the Aztec Empire under the rule of its mighty Moctuzuma.

After disembarking his flotilla at Villa Rica near Vera Cruz, he succeeded in his endeavor, within two and a half months.

Rarely in the annals of warfare history, has there been such a triumphant saga of a military campaign in foreign lands, victorious against all odds.

Of course, the fire-spitting cannons with their deadly balls, swordsmen, archers, and muske-teers in tight formations and fourteen combat-trained horses spearheading the surprise attack with flaring nostrils, front legs high in the air and the riders flaying their swords to the left and right—a sight never before seen—scared the living daylights out of the Aztec warriors. Though well trained but comparatively poorly equipped in armament, they were panic-stricken to flee in a disarrayed retreat to defeat.

It is a long and most interesting story to read about in detail, as so vividly told in a book written by Bernal Diaz, who at age seventeen joined Cortés's expeditionary forces and actually partook in this entire episode to the bitter end to follow.

To me, it would be a Mexico much heard and read about but never visited before, except for the short interlude of the bullfight in Tijuana.

I became totally engrossed with Mexico's history and particularly that of the Mayan generation in Yucatán.

We started out by following Cortés's path leading from Villa Rica to the conquest of Tenochtitlán, the original site of present-day Mexico City, now the capital of Mexico. However, in those ancient days it was a well-fortified island city, crisscrossed by waterways in a geometric pattern and only two major causeways leading into the center of the city.

The huge main plaza was surrounded by a grouping of brilliant colored pyramid-temples and palaces for the emperor and ruling aristocracy, loaded with caches of gold and priceless treasures. It was an unexpected surprise even to the most jaded eyes of some of the Spanish intruders. To get rich that's what they came for primarily and secondary to convert the heathen populace to Catholicism, to please King Charles II of Spain.

Long before the Aztecs arrived in the broad valley of Tenochtitlán (Mexico City today), the Olmecs and Toltecs, had firmly established themselves in this part of the country. Much of their culture blended itself into the future rise to prominence of the Aztec dynasty.

There were also the Maya people in Yucatán, who had already reached a higher plateau of cultural and architectural endeavors.

Chichén Itzá and Uxmal, exceptionally well preserved and partially restored are an archaeologist's dream fulfilled.

Three of the four Atlantes remnants of a Toltec Temple at Tula.

(left)

The jaguar revered as an important deity with temple of Kukulcán (El Castillo) in background.

(right)

The Jaguar Caper

It was brought to my attention that in the very center of the El Castillo Pyramid there was a secret burial chamber, accessible by a steep and narrow staircase. In it there was a carved red jaguar inlaid with green spots of jade and considered one of the finest Aztec treasures. Naturally, I wanted to get at it.

Accompanied by a guard we gained access to the staircase and hauled our Mitchel camera, heavy tripod, four lights with stands, and a small generator to the gated entrance. To my surprise it was blocked like a prison cell with iron bars and a padlock the size of a workman's fist.

I explained to the guard that there was no way for us to light and shoot this jaguar through the iron bars and that we had to have the door opened to let us in. "Is not possible, no key," the guard said. "Then go and get the key," I suggested. "Not possible," he repeated. Remembering a magic word to solve such a dilemma: *mordida*.

I folded a banknote in the palm of my hand and unobtrusively passed it to the guard's hand.

"I try find key," whereupon he left but returned in a suspiciously short time, which only proved to me that he had the key in his pocket all the time.

The gate was opened and as I approached the larger-than-life jaguar, I realized that it was indeed a unique masterpiece of its kind, over a thousand years old and in perfect condition.

In view of the confined space of the chamber, I implored our crewmembers to be most careful in setting up the camera and lights. But even so, one of our hired Mexican electricians, in juggling an obstreperous light stand into position, slightly brushed the jaguar with his back turned toward it. To my horror he knocked out its sharply pointed left incisor. It plopped down close to my right foot.

Momentarily stunned and trying to think what to do next, I shot a glance at the guard a few steps away, luckily absorbed in negoti-

ating with our unit manager an added bonus to his financial windfall. Nonchalantly, I bent over as though I had dropped something, picked up the tooth and while rising turned my back toward the guard to block his view of the jaguar's head. In the nick of time, with a gentle shove I pushed the tooth back into its original orifice. To my great relief it stayed put.

Expediently and even more carefully we got our shot and cleared

out posthaste, without anyone having noticed the tense moments of my sleight of hand dental manipulation.

As the door closed with the padlock snapped shut, I took a parting look at the jaguar's snarling mien. I had a fleeting vision of being arrested and incarcerated for desecration of a religious idol, being fully cognizant of the reputed shortcomings of Mexican jails, in regard to lack of creature comforts an inadequate nourishment.

A love seat appropriately built for two in Mérída.

(above left)

Mayan youngsters perfecting their knowledge in writing, reading, and 'rythmatic.'
Also not to forget the spelling in Nahuatl, their native lingo, of such words as Quetzalcoatl the plumed serpent god, considered "the essence of life." Then there is a temple ruin near Tula by the name of Tlahuizcalpantecuhtli and the charm of Tzintzuntzan, the hummingbird temple.

(below left)

Balloon vendor at Querétaro, Mexico
Young Mayan C.E.O. running his own successful business, while still finding time to peruse the comics.

(right)

Pyramid at Uxmal

To my knowledge the only
existing elliptically designed
pyramid temple in the world,
among historical structures
of this kind.

(left)

Los Voladores de Paplanta

The Aztec equivalent of Canada's
Cirque du Soleil, with four
acrobats attached to a sturdy
rope about to take flight around
an eighty-two-foot-high pole.

Alas, to my everlasting embar-
rassment, I ran out of film in my
camera, without a spare roll on
hand to complete the reportage.
Rest assured it was spectacular.

(right)

San Blas

The Cuná Indians living on an island off the coast of Panama have managed to hold on to the traditions of their forefathers.

The women have cornered the market with the production of their minutely designed and meticulously stitched *Mola* fabrics.

(left)

Ring around the rosy. Children dancing the San Blas way.

(right)

Grape harvest at Undorraga.
Vineyards near Santiago, the
capital of Chile.

(left)

Fishing fleet at Puerto Montt.
Sorting out the morning's catch
in southern Chile.

(above)

Chapter Five

Australia, as a continent is well worth visiting. In fact it is fascinating.

My only regret is that I was under such pressure of a tight schedule, shooting a documentary entitled *Destination South Pacific*. It included, Fiji, New Zealand, Singapore, and Thailand.

Australia has come a long way from the time it began as a penal colony for British convicts.

I found Australia and its people to be a vigorous nation, enterprising and courageous. They'll come through with flying colors staging the 2000 Summer Olympics.

There is one moment that stands out vividly in my memory, when on the morning of November 22, 1963, staying at the Chelsea Hotel in Sydney, a waiter brought my breakfast tray to my room handing me the morning paper and said, "There's bad news for you, sir."

The headline in large letters read: "President John F. Kennedy Assassinated."

It put a damper on the remainder of my prolonged journey.

New Zealand with its North and South Island, is one of nature's wonderlands. They offer everything one could wish for, streams and lakes, mountains to climb, and alpine terrain to ski on. It is an El Dorado for fishermen and sailors to test their seamanship in boats of varied sizes, including the sleek and totally up to date World Cup Racing Yachts.

For the dedicated volcanologist, it is a ready-made observatory of highly active thermal activities, spouting geysers, and erupting volcanoes.

Australia

Looking at Melbourne today,
one might think they returned
to England, to a small town on
the Thames River.

Of course, where there is an
English tradition a jolly game
of cricket is a given.

(below right)

Milford Sound
One of the many idyllic fjords at
the South Island.

(left)

Pohutu Geyser
Near Rotorua at the North
Island, erupting every forty-five
minutes or thereabouts.

(right)

The Maoris. a tribe of Polynesian origin, were the earliest settlers in New Zealand. before the English took over and colonized the country.

Although a respected minority today, the Maoris stick to their proud heritage of culture and mores of their ancestors.

A Maori youth in a choreographed ceremonial greeting to welcome a first-time visitor to their compound.

Maoris are very adept wood-
carvers of larger-than-life statues
of fierce warriors of yore.

Stone Age native primping
and checking the last details
of his "makeup."

(left)

New Guinea warrior all done up
and ready for action, whatever
it may be.

(right)

New Guinea: The Land That Time Forgot was the title of a documentary film I directed for Lowell Thomas in 1972.
At that time there were still undiscovered pockets with hidden tribes that had never seen a white man and cannibalism was a desirable source of nourishment, especially if it was a tasty missionary or young Australian district officer.

We made our headquarters at Mt. Hagen, staying in a primitive hotel or shooting on location in native thatched roof huts with a noticeable lack of elementary frills.
The main attraction of our film was to be a gigantic "Sing-Sing," where about 50,000 natives from the farthest corners of the countryside would gather once a year at Mt. Hagen, to visit, dance and frolic together.

Also at the same time the Australian government would expose them to the latest progress of "civilization," made in faraway countries.
To Lowell, and my younger son Mark, who accompanied me, it was the experience of a lifetime. In fact, for Mark having come halfway around the world, I arranged for him to circle the globe on his own, after the job was finished.

When we met again back at home two months later, I asked him, "Now that you have seen so much of the beauty of this planet, ancient civilizations and glamorous cities, where would you wish to return, if offered to do so?"
His answer, "New Guinea!"

A last practice before the
"Big Sing-Sing" at Mt. Hagen.

(above)

The family that bathes together,
stays clean together.

(right)

When I took this picture, a
smile came to my face, thinking
of Franz Schubert's lovely song
"Das Mädchen am Spinnrad" (The
Maiden on the Spinning Wheel).

(left)

The wealth of a New Guinea
native is counted by the number
of pigs he owns. It's like money
in the bank to barter with. This
one, neatly bundled up, is on its
way to be traded for something
else at the market.

(above right)

Wherever there is a "Sing-Sing"
the mummy of the chief, accompanied by an honor guard, is carried
along as a propitious omen.

(below right)

North America

After wandering around the globe for nine decades, I'll take the continent of North America as the ultimate choice for a life's fulfillment.

Never have there been more meaningful words written, than the ones in paragraph two of our Declaration of Independence.

"We hold these truths to be self-evident that all men are created equal, that they are endowed by their creator with certain unalienable rights, that among these are life, liberty and the pursuit of happiness."

That's what America is all about and I am proud to be one of its citizens.

Our country is blessed with nature's scenic wonders and man-made accomplishments of the highest order. It has everything one could wish for such as oceans, large lakes, mighty rivers, vast fertile plains, and immense forest holdings. It has mountains to rival the European Alps, deserts as barren as the Sahara, and a climate from salubrious to arctic temperatures.

So much has been accomplished in these past 200 years and much is still left to be done. It will be done with patience, perseverance, and the will of the people to husband our country's resources.

Here are a few glimpses of images that caught my attention.

Chapter Six

Two of the most important
landmarks connected in the
development of my two careers.
One as a director of ski schools
and the other as a filmmaker.

Majestic Mt. Rainier
near Seattle, Washington.

(left)

Skier-friendly Mt. Baldy
at Sun Valley, Idaho.

(above)

The Woodland Park Zoo in Seattle, well known for its visionary novel display of exotic animals, without restricting cages, provided me with this striking image of a "Silver Back" Mountain Gorilla. *(left)*

If you should wish to go to Africa avoiding the long journey and costly airfare, I suggest Safari West in Sonoma County, near Santa Rosa, California. It is owned and managed by my older son Peter and his wife Nancy; both dedicated conservationists.

Through a decade of hard work they have nurtured and developed this game preserve into an authentic African tent camp, luxuriously appointed for overnight stays. There are scheduled safaris by appointment in rugged vehicles cruising the 300 acres of undulating terrain, to view a variety of African species, some of these on the endangered list of extinction. Here they are grazing and breeding peacefully, without being threatened by dangerous carnivores.

It is a photographer's field day, such as capturing Delilah, a show-off hornbill, roosting regally high up on a shady tree limb but conveniently descending

to feast on her specially prepared meal, while graciously posing for a photograph.

There are gazelles, zebras, antelopes, and scimitar horned oryx within close reach of the safari vehicle, accompanied by a knowledgeable guide.

Here is also the giraffe I used as a "stand-in double" for the original Zarafa, the one who captured the imagination of France and the world by her adventurous journey from Africa to Paris.

Now this giraffe has a baby daughter of her own, also named Zarafa.

Zarafa then and there—Zarafa here and now, it get's a bit complicated in this world of ours.*

* *Zarafa: A Giraffe's True Story* by
   Michael Allin. Published by Walker
   and Company, New York, NY

Potted gloxinia, photographed
against an oil painting for
a background.

(left)

Butchart Gardens, Victoria, B.C.
Since I could not afford to
buy an original Monet, I thought
the next best thing would be
to concoct one with my camera.

(right)

Indian Reservation,
La Push, Washington
I had hoped to find something
like a picturesque fishing village
on the coast of Normandy in
France, but only wound up with
one single shot worth taking,
while waiting for a gas station
to open.

(left)

West Seattle, Washington
Totem pole made entirely of
driftwood pieces, one among
many others created by Albert
Salisbury, writer and artist
emeritus, a.k.a. "Alki Al."

(right)

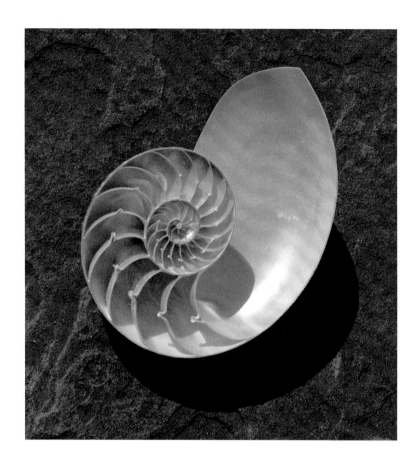

Nautilus Shell
One of nature's most
perfect designs.

(left)

Abstract sculpture, acrylic
on stainless steel plate.
Artist: Jack Chandler
Calistoga, California.
The hammock was hung
for a convenient "siesta."

(right)

Arizona, U.S.A.
Zuni Indian family at work
and play.

(above)

Albuquerque, New Mexico
"Balloon Fiesta," a gathering of
balloons by the hundreds of all
shapes and sizes.

(left)

West Seattle, Washington
Statue of Liberty at Alki Beach,
where the first settlers arrived
from New England and the
growth of Seattle began.
Many of the streets and buildings
in this city are named in honor
of the original settlers.

(left)

The ever-changing view from
my writer's den, looking down
at Alki Beach, across Puget
Sound, Bainbridge Island, and
the Olympic Mountain Range.
It looks deceptively like a
miniature panorama of the
Himalayas with Mt. Everest
in the center.

(right)

Tehachapi, California
Roundup time at
Stallion Springs.
(left)

Death Valley, California
Borax mule wagon detail.
(right)

Washington

Lake Crescent, Olympic Rain
Forest National Park.

(left)

Marymere Falls, Olympic Rain
Forest National Park.

(right)

Ice Palace, Jackson, Wyoming
The fine spray of a running water hose, windblown and frozen into this formation of an abstract ice sculpture.

(left)

"King of the Summit." Top of Crystal Mountain with Mt. Rainier in the background. According to Audubon the bird is identified as Clark's Nutcracker, colloquially better known as "Camp Robber" with no further comment.

(right)

Tacoma. Washington
Refurbished Union Station in
Tacoma. with Chihuly's glass-
blown flowers. floating like
butterflies in the night sky.

(left)

A wanderer all packed and
ready to go. Could it be me?
Where to. that is the question.
with an open road to new hori-
zons beckoning. so temptingly.

(right)

Antarctica

To me, the continent of Antarctica remains terra incognita—for the time being.

All I know is, that it is the most isolated and unfit living place on earth, with temperatures sinking to -74° F. Plus an added chill factor of winds at 200 miles and a continent in pitch darkness for about six months of the year.

Antarctica belongs to no single nation, but approximately thirteen countries have staked out claims on small pie-shaped slices of inhospitable terrain for scientific research. The U.S.A. camp at McMurdo is the largest and best-equipped outpost of the lot.

Who can tell sometime, someday, maybe I could still bum myself a ride to Antarctica to complete my cycle *Around the World in 90 Years!*

Chapter Seven

There is a variety of the penguin
species inhabiting Antarctica
by multiple thousands,
notwithstanding the severity
of the arctic climate.

They are also favorites with the
public at the Woodland Park Zoo
in Seattle, cavorting about under
balmier weather conditions.